# The My Lai Massacre: The History of the Vietnam War's Most Notorious Atrocity

By Charles River Editors

Picture of an American soldier setting fire to a dwelling during the massacre

## About Charles River Editors

**Charles River Editors** provides superior editing and original writing services across the digital publishing industry, with the expertise to create digital content for publishers across a vast range of subject matter. In addition to providing original digital content for third party publishers, we also republish civilization's greatest literary works, bringing them to new generations of readers via ebooks.

Sign up here to receive updates about free books as we publish them, and visit Our Kindle Author Page to browse today's free promotions and our most recently published Kindle titles.

## Introduction

**Victims of the massacre**

# My Lai

"I walked up and saw these guys doing strange things...Setting fire to the hootches and huts and waiting for people to come out and then shooting them...going into the hootches and shooting them up...gathering people in groups and shooting them... As I walked in you could see piles of people all through the village... all over. They were gathered up into large groups. I saw them shoot an M79 [grenade launcher] into a group of people who were still alive. But it was mostly done with a machine gun. They were shooting women and children just like anybody else. We met no resistance and I only saw three captured weapons. We had no casualties. It was just like any other Vietnamese village-old papa-sans, women and kids. As a matter of fact, I don't remember seeing one military-age male in the entire place, dead or alive." - PFC Michael Bernhardt

The Vietnam War could have been called a comedy of errors if the consequences weren't so deadly and tragic. In 1951, while war was raging in Korea, the United States began signing defense pacts with nations in the Pacific, intending to create alliances that would contain the spread of Communism. As the Korean War was winding down, America joined the Southeast Asia Treaty Organization, pledging to defend several nations in the region from Communist aggression. One of those nations was South Vietnam.

Before the Vietnam War, most Americans would have been hard pressed to locate Vietnam on a map. South Vietnamese President Diem's regime was extremely unpopular, and war broke out between Communist North Vietnam and South Vietnam around the end of the 1950s. Kennedy's administration tried to prop up the South Vietnamese with training and assistance, but the South Vietnamese military was feeble. A month before his death, Kennedy signed a presidential directive withdrawing 1,000 American personnel, and shortly after Kennedy's assassination, new President Lyndon B. Johnson reversed course, instead opting to expand American assistance to South Vietnam.

The Tet Offensive made President Johnson non-credible and historically unpopular, and he did not run for reelection in 1968. By then, Vietnam had already fueled the hippie counterculture, and anti-war protests spread across the country. On campuses and in the streets, some protesters spread peace and love, but others rioted. In August 1968, riots broke out in the streets of Chicago, as the National Guard and police took on 10,000 anti-war rioters during the Democratic National Convention.

The Vietnam War remains one of the most controversial events in American history, and it bitterly divided the nation in 1968, but it could have been far worse. That's because, unbeknownst to most Americans that year, American forces had carried out the most notorious mass killing of the war that March. On March 16, perhaps as many as 500 Vietnamese villagers in the Son My village complex - men, women, and children - were killed by American soldiers in Task Force Barker. The worst of the violence, carried out by members of Charlie Company, 1st Battalion, 11th Infantry, occurred in a small village known locally as Xom Lang. On American maps, the location was marked as My Lai (4), and when news of the killings leaked into the American press over a year and a half later in November 1969, it was under that name that the incident became infamous as the "My Lai Massacre."

The My Lai Massacre was possibly the single worst atrocity committed by American forces during the long and sometimes brutal Vietnam War, and it has been called "the most shocking episode of the Vietnam War." It became a touchstone not only for the controversial conflict but for the manner in which the American government had covered up the truth, which many felt was emblematic of the government's behavior throughout much of the war itself. Moreover, it damaged the nation's credibility, as well as the military's; as Reinhold Neibuhr put it, "I think there is a good deal of evidence that we thought all along that we were a redeemer nation. There was a lot of illusion in our national history. Now it is about to be shattered."

By the end of the decade, Vietnam had left tens of thousands of Americans dead, spawned a counterculture with millions of protesters, and destroyed a presidency, and more was still yet to come. As David H. Hackworth put it, "Vietnam was an atrocity from the get-go... There were hundreds of My Lais. You got your card punched by the numbers of bodies you counted."

As for My Lai itself, with the exceptions of veterans and their families, American memories of the Vietnam conflict have grown increasingly hazy. Few younger people today even recognize the name My Lai, and in its own way, communist Vietnam has also moved on. For those who were in My Lai that day, however, the wounds will always be fresh.

*The My Lai Massacre: The History of the Vietnam War's Most Notorious Atrocity* traces the history of one of the American military's darkest days. Along with pictures of important people, places, and events, you will learn about My Lai like never before, in no time at all.

The My Lai Massacre: The History of the Vietnam War's Most Notorious Atrocity

About Charles River Editors

Introduction

   Chapter 1: Heading for War

   Chapter 2: Escalation

   Chapter 3: The Experience of War

   Chapter 4: Charlie Company

   Chapter 5: The Plan

   Chapter 6: The My Lai Massacre

   Chapter 7: The Aftermath of My Lai

   Pictures of the Massacre Taken by Ronald Haeberle

   Online Resources

   Bibliography

## Chapter 1: Heading for War

By March 1968, the United States had been heavily invested in opposing Vietnamese communism for the better part of two decades, and with the benefit of hindsight, the American war effort that metastasized there throughout the 1960s may seem like a grievous error and a needless waste of blood and treasure on an unwinnable and strategically insignificant civil conflict in a distant, culturally alien land. Indeed, it is still difficult for Americans today to comprehend how it was that their leaders determined such a course was in the national interest. Thus, it is essential at the outset to inquire how it was that a succession of elite American politicians, bureaucrats, and military officers managed, often despite their own inherent skepticism, to convince both themselves and the public that a communist Vietnam would constitute a grave threat to America's security.

Vietnam's first modern revolution came in the months of violence, famine, and chaos that succeeded World War II in Asia. Along with present-day Laos and Cambodia, the country had been a French colony since the late 19th century, but more recently, at the outset of World War II, the entire region had been occupied by the Japanese. Despite the pan-Asian anti-colonialism they publicly espoused, Japan did little to alter the basic structures of political and economic control the French had erected.

When Japan surrendered and relinquished all claim to its overseas empire, spontaneous uprisings occurred in Hanoi, Hue, and other Vietnamese cities. These were seized upon by the Vietnam Independence League (or *Vietminh*) and its iconic leader Ho Chi Minh, who declared an independent Democratic Republic of Vietnam (DRV) on September 2, 1945. France, which had reoccupied most of the country by early 1946, agreed in theory to grant the DRV limited autonomy. However, when the sharp limits of that autonomy became apparent, the Vietminh took up arms. By the end of 1946, in the first instance of what would become a longstanding pattern, the French managed to retain control of the cities while the rebels held sway in the countryside.

**Ho Chi Minh**

From the outset, Ho hoped to avoid conflict with the United States. He was a deeply committed Communist and dedicated to class warfare and social revolution, but at the same time, he was also a steadfast Vietnamese nationalist who remained wary of becoming a puppet of the Soviet Union or the People's Republic of China. Indeed, Ho's very real popularity throughout the country rested to no small extent on his ability to tap into a centuries-old popular tradition of national resistance against powerful foreign hegemons, a tradition originally directed against imperial China. As such, he made early advances to Washington, even deliberately echoing the American Declaration of Independence in his own declaration of Vietnamese independence.

Under different circumstances, Americans might not have objected much to a communist but independent DRV. The Roosevelt and Truman administrations had trumpeted national independence in Asia and exhibited almost nothing but contempt for French colonial rule. However, as Cold War tensions rose, and as the Soviet Union and (after 1949) Communist China increased their material and rhetorical support for the Vietminh cause, such subtle gradations quickly faded. Considering the matter in May 1949, Secretary of State Dean Acheson asserted that the question of whether Ho was "as much nationalist as Commie is irrelevant. All Stalinists in colonial areas are nationalists . . . Once in power their objective necessarily becomes subordination [of the] state to Commie purpose." (Young, 20 – 23).

**Acheson**

As a result, in 1950, the United States recognized the new puppet government France had established under the emperor Bao Dai, and by 1953 American financial aid funded fully 60% of France's counterinsurgency effort. When that effort finally collapsed in 1954, an international conference at Geneva agreed to divide Vietnam at the 17th parallel into a communist DRV in the north and an American-backed Republic of Vietnam in the south. Between 1955 and 1961, South Vietnam and its new president, Ngo Dinh Diem, received more than $1 billion in American aid. Even so, Diem proved unable to consolidate support for his regime, and by 1961 he faced a growing insurgency in the Viet Cong (VC), a coalition of local guerilla groups supported and directed by North Vietnam.

Diem

**Bao Dai**

As Diem and (after a 1963 coup) his successors teetered on the brink of disaster, American politicians and military officers grappled with the difficult question of how much they were willing to sacrifice to support an ally. In 1961, President Kennedy resisted a push to mount air strikes, but he agreed to send increased financial aid to South Vietnam, along with hundreds (and eventually thousands) of American "military advisors."

**Chapter 2: Escalation**

"The last thing I wanted to do was to be a wartime President." – Lyndon B. Johnson

The summer of 1964, which would normally be used to prepare for reelection, was a busy time for Lyndon B. Johnson's Administration. His attempts to steamroll ahead on domestic policy legislation were quickly sideswiped by a surprising foreign policy event: the Gulf of Tonkin incident. In 1964, the *USS Maddox* was an intelligence-gathering naval ship stationed off the coast of North Vietnam for the purpose of gathering information about the ongoing conflict between North Vietnam and South Vietnam. The borders between North and South, however, were in dispute, and the United States was less up to date on changes in these borders than the two belligerents. In the process, the *USS Maddox* accidentally crossed over into North Vietnamese shores, and when the ship was sighted by North Vietnamese naval units, they attacked the *Maddox* on August 2, 1964.

Though no Americans were hurt, naval crews were on heightened alert as the *Maddox* retreated to South Vietnam, where it was met by the USS *Turner Joy*. Two days later, the *Maddox* and *Turner Joy*, both with crews already on edge as a result of the events of August 2, were certain they were being followed by hostile North Vietnamese boats, and both fired at targets popping up on their radar.

After this second encounter, Johnson gave a speech over radio to the American people shortly before midnight on August 4th. He told of attacks on the high seas, suggesting the events occurred in international waters, and vowed the nation would be prepared for its own defense and the defense of the South Vietnamese. Johnson thus had the Gulf of Tonkin Resolution drafted, which gave the right of military preparedness to the President without Congressional approval. The resolution passed shortly thereafter, giving the President the authority to raise military units in Vietnam and engage in warfare as needed without any consent from Congress. Shortly thereafter, President Johnson approved air strikes against the North Vietnamese, and Congress approved military action with the Gulf of Tonkin Resolution.

Once upon a time, Johnson had claimed, "We are not about to send American boys 9 or 10 thousand miles away from home to do what Asian boys ought to be doing for themselves." By the end of the year, however, over 16,000 Americans were stationed in South Vietnam. Regarding this about-face, Johnson would explain, "Just like the Alamo, somebody damn well needed to go to their aid. Well, by God, I'm going to Vietnam's aid!"

It would be years before the government revealed that the second encounter was no encounter at all. The government never figured out what the *Maddox* and *Turner Joy* were firing at that night, but there was no indication that it involved the North Vietnamese. Regardless, by 1965, under intense pressure from his advisors and with regular units of the North Vietnamese Army (NVA) infiltrating into the south, President Lyndon Johnson reluctantly agreed to a bombing campaign, Operation Rolling Thunder, against North Vietnamese targets. He also agreed to a request from General William Westmoreland, the American military commander in South Vietnam, for the first American ground troops deployed to Vietnam: two battalions of Marines to guard the air bases.

**Westmoreland**

Over the next few years, the American military commitment to South Vietnam grew dramatically, and the war effort became both deeper and more complex. The strategy included parallel efforts to strengthen the economic and political foundations of the South Vietnamese regime, to root out the Viet Cong guerilla insurgency in the south, combat the more conventional NVA near the Demilitarized Zone between north and south, and bomb military and industrial targets in North Vietnam itself. In public, American military officials and members of the Johnson administration stressed their tactical successes and offered rosy predictions; speaking before the National Press Club in November 1967, General Westmoreland claimed, "I am absolutely certain that whereas in 1965 the enemy was winning, today he is certainly losing." (*New York Times*, November 22, 1967).

At the same time, the government worked to conceal from the American public their own doubts and the grim realities of war. Reflecting on the willful public optimism of American officials at the time, Colonel Harry G. Summers concluded, "We in the military knew better, but through fear of reinforcing the basic antimilitarism of the American people we tended to keep this knowledge to ourselves and downplayed battlefield realities . . . We had concealed from the American people the true nature of the war." (Summers, 63).

By the end of 1967, with nearly half a million troops deployed, more than 19,000 deaths, and a war that cost $2 billion a month and seemed to grow bloodier by the day, the Johnson administration faced an increasingly impatient and skeptical nation. Early in 1968, a massive coordinated Viet Cong operation - the Tet Offensive - briefly paralyzed American and South Vietnamese forces across the country, threatening even the American embassy compound in Saigon. With this, the smiling mask slipped even further, inflaming the burgeoning antiwar movement.

Years later, General Fred C. Weyland speculated that the disingenuous pronouncements of officers and politicians, while instrumental in making the initial case for intervention, may have poisoned the well of long-term public support: "The American way of war is particularly violent, deadly and dreadful. We believe in using 'things'—artillery, bombs, massive firepower—in order to conserve our soldiers' lives. The enemy, on the other hand, made up for his lack of 'things' by expending men instead of machines, and he suffered enormous casualties. The army saw this happen in Korea, and we should have made the realities of war obvious to the American people before they witnessed it on their television screens. The army must make the price of involvement clear before we get involved." (Summers, 68).

Whether greater openness from the outset might have translated into steadier national resolve in the long term is impossible to say, but it would almost certainly have punctured some of the dangerous illusions that young American soldiers brought with them to Vietnam.

**Chapter 3: The Experience of War**

Compared with their predecessors in World War II and Korea, the average American soldier in Vietnam was considerably younger and in many cases came from more marginal economic backgrounds. The average American soldier in World War II was 26, but in Vietnam, the average soldier was barely 19. In part, this was due to President Johnson's refusal to mobilize the national reserves; concerned that calling up the National Guard would spook the public and possibly antagonize the Russians or Chinese, Johnson relied on the draft to fill the ranks of the military.

In all, between 1964 and 1973, fully 2.2 million American men were drafted into the military, and an additional 8.7 million enlisted voluntarily, or at least semi-voluntarily. Knowing that draftees were more likely to be assigned to combat roles, many men who expected to be drafted took the initiative to enlist in the military before the Selective Service Board had a chance to call them up. This was a risky bet, perhaps, but not necessarily a crazy one, because enlistees were less than half as likely as draftees to be killed in Vietnam.

Moreover, given the numerous Selective Service deferments available for attending college, being married, holding a defense-related job, or serving in the National Guard, the burden of the draft fell overwhelmingly on the people from working class backgrounds. It also particularly affected African Americans.

The American military that these young draftees and enlistees joined had been forged in the crucible of World War II and were tempered by two decades of Cold War with the Soviet Union. In terms of its organization, equipment, training regimens, operational doctrines, and its very outlook, the American military was designed to fight a major conventional war against a similarly-constituted force, whether in Western Europe or among the plains of northeast Asia. As an organization, the military's collective memories were of just such engagements at places like Midway, Normandy, Iwo Jima, Incheon, and the Battle of the Bulge. These campaigns predominately involved battles of infantry against infantry, tanks against tanks, and jet fighters against jet fighters. As boys, many of the young men who fought in Vietnam had played as soldiers, re-enacting the heroic tales of their fathers and grandfathers. The author Philip Caputo, who arrived in Vietnam as a young marine officer in 1965, recalled, "I saw myself charging up some distant beachhead, like John Wayne in *Sands of Iwo Jima*, and then coming home with medals on my chest." (Caputo, 6).

Expecting a simple conflict of good against evil and knowing little to nothing of the local culture, American soldiers in their late teens and early twenties arrived in Vietnam and found a world of peril, privation, and moral ambiguity. Despairing of and for young rookie soldiers like Caputo, Bruce Lawler, a CIA case officer in South Vietnam, virtually exploded with rage: "How in hell can you put people like that into a war? How can you inject these types of guys into a situation that requires a tremendous amount of sophistication? You can't. What happens is they start shooting at anything that moves because they don't know. They're scared. I mean, they're out there getting shot at, and Christ, there's somebody with eyes that are different from mine. And boom—it's gone." (Saltoli, 177).

Indeed, with a few notable exceptions, the American military experience in Vietnam consisted largely of small-scale encounters. Understanding full well that contesting a conventional battle with the better-armed Americans amounted to committing suicide, the Viet Cong waged an asymmetrical guerilla-style campaign that capitalized on their superior knowledge of the terrain, their closer relations with local villagers, and their deeper commitment to the cause. Viet Cong guerillas wore no uniforms, did not always bear their arms openly, did not observe traditional battle lines, and blended in with the villagers who supported them. During the war, an American soldier was as likely to be killed by a land mine, a booby trap, or a hidden sniper as by an enemy he could see.

To the Viet Cong themselves, such tactics were natural and justified in a "people's war": "The soldiers came from the people. They were the children of the villagers. The villagers loved them, protected them, fed them. They were the people's soldiers." (FitzGerald, 201). To the Americans, however, the insurgents seemed sneaky and treacherous, readier to hide behind women and children than to stand and fight like men.

Of course, such guerrilla tactics served to blur the lines between combatant and civilian. As Specialist 4th Class Fred Widmer of Charlie Company explained, "The same village you had gone in to give them medical treatment . . . you could go through that village later and get shot at on your way out by a sniper. Go back in, you wouldn't find anybody. Nobody knew anything . . . You didn't trust them anymore." (Widmer).

Faced with such a determined opponent, skilled in asymmetrical warfare and enjoying considerable popular support, General Westmoreland chose to fight a war of attrition. While he did employ strategic hamlets, pacification programs, and other kinetic counterinsurgency operations, he largely relied on his massive advantage in firepower to overwhelm and grind down the Viet Cong and NVA in South Vietnam. The goal was simple: to reach a "crossover point" at which communist fighters were being killed more quickly than they could be replaced. American ground forces would lure the enemy into the open, where they would be destroyed by a combination of artillery and air strikes.

Naturally, if American soldiers on the ground often had trouble distinguishing combatants from civilians, B-52 bombers flying at up to 30,000 feet were wholly indiscriminate when targeting entire villages. By the end of 1966, American bombers and fighter-bombers in Vietnam dropped about 825 tons of explosive every day, more than all the bombs dropped on Europe during World War II. As Secretary of Defense Robert McNamara wrote to President Johnson in May of 1967, "The picture of the world's greatest superpower killing or seriously injuring 1,000 noncombatants a week, while trying to pound a tiny backward nation into submission on an issue whose merits are hotly disputed, is not a pretty one." (Sheehan, 685).

By 1968, civilian casualties in South Vietnam were estimated to be at least 300,000 per year, and Westmoreland has often been criticized for employing such a brutal and ultimately ineffective strategy. In fairness, however, it must be noted that he had few genuinely attractive options. Seeking out a decisive victory by invading the north had been ruled out by the Johnson administration as too provocative since it was likely to pull China or the Soviet Union into the war, but Westmoreland's troops were too few, too young, and too inexperienced to carry out a full counterinsurgency as the British had in Malaya. As Westmoreland later argued, "Had I at my disposal virtually unlimited manpower, I could have stationed troops permanently in every district or province and thus provided an alternative strategy. That would have enabled the troops to get to know the people intimately, facilitating the task of identifying the subversives and protecting the others against intimidation. Yet to have done that would have required literally millions of men." (Westmoreland).

This may well be so, but it is difficult to deny that the strategy of attrition - and the largely indiscriminate means used to achieve it - were bound to drive a wedge between the American military and even anti-communist civilians. "Search and destroy" missions sought to eliminate not only VC guerillas but also any food, shelter, or materials they might use. Westmoreland and the Military Assistance Command, Vietnam (MACV) declared large swathes of South Vietnam as "free fire" zones, meaning villages in these zones could be carpet bombed and civilians were automatically considered enemy combatants.

Above all, success was measured in terms of "body count;" Westmoreland's staff estimated the crossover point at a kill ratio of 10 Viet Cong to every American. To that end, officers rewarded soldiers for confirmed kills, rules of engagement were unofficially loosened, and operations were sometimes planned solely to increase the body count. As Philip Caputo notes, the consequences of such a strategy for the outlook of the ordinary American soldier were as tragic as they were predictable: "General Westmoreland's strategy of attrition also had an important effect on our behavior. Our mission was not to win terrain or seize positions, but simply to kill: to kill Communists and to kill as many of them as possible. Stack 'em like cordwood. Victory was a high body count, defeat a low kill ratio, war a matter of arithmetic. The pressure on unit commanders to produce enemy corpses was intense, and they in turn communicated it to their troops . . . It is not surprising, therefore, that some men acquired a contempt for human life and a predilection for taking it." (Caputo, xix).

**Chapter 4: Charlie Company**

"I was ordered to go in there and destroy the enemy. That was my job that day. That was the mission I was given. I did not sit down and think in terms of men, women, and children. They were all classified as the same, and that's the classification that we dealt with over there, just as the enemy. I felt then and I still do that I acted as I was directed, and I carried out the order that I was given and I do not feel wrong in doing so." - Lieutenant William L. Calley, Jr.

Charlie Company, the single most analyzed army unit in American history, was a component of the 1st Battalion, 20th Infantry, of the 11th Brigade, of the Americal Division. The division dated back to 1942, when it was patched together from a number of units on New Caledonia (*Americal* is actually a contraction of *American* and *Caledonia*). Members of the division served at Guadalcanal, the Philippines, and were used during the occupation of Japan and in the Panama Canal Zone. After being deactivated, the division was reestablished in September 1967 for combat duty in South Vietnam. Nothing about the division was particularly unusual, though its patchwork nature meant that the brigades making it up sometimes had difficulty adhering to a single division-wide set of procedures and regulations.

**The shoulder sleeve insignia for the 11th Brigade**

Most of the 150 young men who made up Charlie Company joined the army in the second half of 1966 and spent the winter of 1966-67 in basic training. There was little to distinguish them from their fellow soldiers, though they were on average somewhat more likely to have graduated high school. They were largely between 18-22 years old, and about 50% were African American. As the Peers Report would later conclude, "The men were generally representative of the typical cross section of American youth assigned to most combat units throughout the Army . . . [They] brought with them the diverse traits, prejudices and attitudes typical of the various regions of the country and segments of society from whence they came." (Peers Report).

While the men were in basic training, the nucleus of the 1st Battalion, 20th Infantry, a historic but inactive unit, was being re-formed at Schofield Barracks in Hawaii. In December 1966, the small group of officers and NCOs was joined by Captain Ernest Medina, who would command Charlie Company. Medina was a career soldier from a poor Mexican American family who had enlisted in the army as soon as he was old enough and worked his way up to Captain. As a commander, "Mad Dog" Medina was generally respected as stern, energetic, and extremely capable. Within months of their arrival in Hawaii, he had shaped his raw recruits into a highly effective unit, generally recognized as the best in the brigade. Indeed, when the 11th Brigade embarked for Vietnam in December 1967, the honor of serving as advance guard went to Charlie Company.

**Medina**

Lieutenant William L. Calley, Jr. would command Charlie Company's 1st Platoon during the assault on My Lai (4). The only man to be tried over the massacre, he became a hugely controversial figure and a flashpoint in the national controversy over the Vietnam War. At the time he enlisted, however, Calley was a seemingly unremarkable young man from a middle class Miami family. Calley had been a poor student, graduating in the bottom quarter of his high school class and later dropping out of Palm Beach Junior College. In 1964 he attempted to join the Army, but he was rejected after he failed the physical.

**Calley**

For the next two years, Calley drifted across the country working a succession of odd jobs, but in 1966, with a notice from the draft board back in Miami, he enlisted at a local army recruiting station in Albuquerque. He completed basic training at Fort Bliss, Texas, followed by the Adjutant General's Corps course at Fort Lewis, and he seemed likely to continue on as an army clerk, a position far removed from combat, but a superior apparently noticed that he had attended Georgia Military Academy in his youth and thus sent him for officer training at Fort Benning. From there, he was assigned to Schofield Barracks and Medina's Charlie Company. Shortly before deploying for Vietnam, Calley was assigned to lead the company in a class session called "Vietnam Our Host," essentially a short list of "dos and don'ts" designed to help the men maintain good relations with the locals. "Oh God what a farce it was," Calley remembered, "I did a very poor job of it." (Sack, 29).

In early December 1967, Charlie Company arrived at Landing Zone (LZ) Bronco in Quang Ngai, a coastal province in the Republic of Vietnam's north. In Quang Ngai, the company received a few days of orientation and combat assault training, then spent several weeks conducting relatively uneventful short-range patrols. In January 1968, however, the company was assigned to Task Force Barker, about 500 troops patched together from different units of the Americal Division. The force—named for its commander, Lieutenant Colonel Frank Barker—was assigned to the Son Tinh District in the province's north, an area controlled by the Viet Cong 48th Local Force Battalion. Barker's orders were simple: search out and destroy the Viet Cong in the area.

Charlie Company was assigned to LZ Dottie, a well-fortified base northeast of Quang Ngai City surrounded on all sides by VC-controlled countryside. The company played little part in Task Force Barker's first major engagement, an intense battle for control of Quang Ngai City that coincided with the Tet Offensive across South Vietnam. However, once Barker had secured the city and Viet Cong units spread out across the countryside to regroup, Medina and his men were assigned to clear their area, including the village complex of Son My. Repeated patrols in the area turned up few Viet Cong, but the Americans were subjected to sporadic booby traps, mines, and sniper fire. On February 12, Calley led his men across an exposed earthen dike, where Specialist 4th Class William Weber, the company's radio telephone operator, was killed by an unseen sniper, making him Charlie Company's first casualty. The next day, Task Force Barker had its first major engagement with Viet Cong in the area, a three-day fight that left three Americans and 80 Vietnamese dead.

On February 25, while on patrol, members of Charlie Company stumbled into a mine field, and in the chaos, three men were killed and 16 wounded, the company's worst loss yet. Medina, who was with the company at the time, responded coolly, directing medical aid to the wounded while working with mine detectors to clear a safe path out. He was later awarded a silver star for his valor that day. Calley, who had been on leave at the time, returned to LZ Dottie to find his company changed: "It seemed like a different company now." (Hammer, 304 – 05).

It was widely believed that local villagers had known about the mine field but failed to warn the soldiers. "These people are just as much VC as the ones that actually planted those minefields," concluded Lieutenant Roger Alaux, the company's forward artillery observer. (Sack, 73).

In response, members of the company adopted increasingly harsh, suspicious attitudes toward local villagers, even children. Fred Widmer, in a 1992 interview, described the change that he and his fellow soldiers went through this way: "When we first started losing members of the company, it was mostly through booby-traps and snipers. We never really got into a main conflict per se, where you could see who was shooting and you could actually shoot back. We had heard a lot about women and children being used as booby-traps and being members of the Viet Cong. As time went on you tended to believe it more and more. There was no question that they were working for the Viet Cong. But at the same time we were trying to work with these people, they were basically doing a number on us—and we were letting them. So the whole mood changed. You didn't trust them anymore. You didn't trust anybody. Deep down inside, you had mixed emotions. You knew there was an enemy out there—but you couldn't pinpoint who exactly was the enemy. And I would say that in the end, anybody that was still in that country was the enemy." (Widmer).

This turn toward suspicion and antagonism had real consequences for the men of Charlie Company and for the Vietnamese they encountered, whether they were Viet Cong, sympathizers, or ordinary villagers. In fact, allegations of abuse, torture, and outright murder in the weeks leading up to the My Lai massacre were eventually leveled against Charlie Company, though the actual facts are difficult to determine. According to Widmer, atrocities were already frequent and widespread among the men of the company:

"The first time I saw something really bad was the point at which we stopped taking prisoners. We had been there about a month and a half, or two months. There was one guy Medina had shoot the prisoners. Instead of having everyone around and shoot them, they would walk them down toward the beach, or behind some sand dunes, and shoot them—a couple of shots and they were done. As time went by, things were done, ears cut off, mutilations. One prisoner had his arms tied straight out on a stick. One was a woman and one was a man; there was no question that these two were Viet Cong. The woman was working as a nurse and we found them in a tunnel with all the medical supplies and we knew they were the enemy. Lit cigarettes were put inside the elastic of the guy's pants and we watched him dance around because they were burning his ass. I think it was a bit of making him talk and a bit of venting our frustrations, a bit of both. I don't remember what happened to them, whether they were turned over or shot.

"The more it went on, the more you didn't trust anyone; you didn't believe anybody because you didn't know who was who, you didn't know who the enemy was. As we went on, more and more prisoners would be executed. I would say it was a regular occurrence, I did abuse someone—a prisoner—a papa san. I found myself doing the same things that had been going on all along. I found myself caught up in it. We cut his beard off him—this was an insult. A papa san with a beard is considered a wise man, and to cut off their beard was a real sign of disrespect to them.

"You found yourself punching them around, beating them up trying to get them to talk. I never did hit anyone with my rifle. I have taken a knife to them . . . I never tortured anyone to death. I think I probably saw people tortured to death." (Widmer).

Michael Bernhardt, a "tunnel rat" in Charlie Company, outlined a similar transition in a 1988 interview. Something of an outsider, Bernhardt described how the anxiety and isolation the company experienced bred a certain perverse moral sense: "When you're in an infantry company, in an isolated environment like this, the rules of that company are foremost. They're the things that really count. The laws back home don't make any difference. What people think of you back home doesn't matter. What matters is what people here and now think about what you're doing. What matters is how the people around you are going to see you. Killing a bunch of civilians in this way—babies, women, old men, people who were unarmed, helpless—was wrong. Every American would know that. And yet this company sitting out here isolated in this one place didn't see it that way. I'm sure they didn't. The group of people was all that mattered. It was the whole world. What they thought was right was right. And what they thought was wrong was wrong. The definitions for things were turned around. Courage was seem as stupidity. Cowardice was cunning and wariness, and cruelty and brutality were seen sometimes as heroic. That's what it eventually turned into." (Bilton and Sims, 18 – 19).

On March 14, another mine claimed the life of Sergeant George Cox. According to numerous later accounts, the members of Charlie Company were eager for revenge.

**Chapter 5: The Plan**

"They're all VC, now go and get them." – A statement attributed to Medina

On the afternoon of March 15, 1968, Lieutenant Colonel Frank Barker gathered his officers and outlined his plans for the next day's operation to his officers. The group met at Barker's command bunker at LZ Dottie, about 7 miles northwest of their target, Son My. Son My was a complex of about a dozen small villages in a lush, productive agricultural region northeast of Quang Ngai City, and the complex was divided into four administrative regions or "hamlets": Tu Cung, My Lai, My Khe, and Co Luy. Somewhat confusingly, the American and Vietnamese names for the villages differed. To the Americans, My Khe village was My Lai (1) or "Pinkville," My Hoi village was My Khe (4), and Xom Lang and Binh Tay villages were My Lai (4). According to Captain Eugene Kotouc, Barker's intelligence officer, the area was controlled by the Viet Cong 48th Local Force Battalion, headquartered either in My Lai (1) or My Lai (4). Kotouc predicted that the task force would experience "heavy resistance" from both Viet Cong and Viet Cong sympathizers in the area.

**A picture of Co Luy**

In most respects, Barker's plan for Son My was little different from other American search and destroy operations in South Vietnam. The operation would begin with artillery fire to soften up Viet Cong fighters holed up in the village complex. The barrage would also serve to clear preselected landing zones for Charlie and Bravo Companies. Charlie Company would be airlifted in just west of My Lai (4), clear the hamlet, and then proceed east to My Lai (1), where they would rendezvous with Bravo Company, which had moved up along the coast from the south. Together, the two companies would serve to drive Viet Cong in the area north into Alpha Company, installed in a blocking position. Meanwhile, US Navy swift boats would sweep up and down the coast, preventing enemy withdrawal to the east. An aero-scout team from the 123rd Aviation Battalion would do the same along Route 521, which ran south of the villages.

Importantly, Koutoc informed Charlie and Bravo companies that by the time they arrived at their landing zones, most genuine villagers would already be well on their way to market. Thus, those remaining in the area could be assumed to be Viet Cong, not innocent civilians. According to Koutoc, Barker then specified that he "wanted the area cleaned out, he wanted it neutralized, and he wanted the buildings knocked down." Colonel Oran K. Henderson, the 11th Brigade's new commander, pushed his officers to move quickly and maximize their confirmed kills and equipment captures. In Captain Medina's words, "He emphasized that he wanted the troops to be aware of this and that they should be aggressive in closing with and destroying the enemy." He also reminded the officers that the Viet Cong sometimes employed women and children to help them escape and to spirit away their weapons and equipment. "When we get through with that 48th Battalion," he concluded, "they won't be giving us any more trouble. We're going to do them once and for all." (Peers report).

Later that day, the members of Charlie Company gathered for an emotional memorial service for Sergeant Cox. Captain Medina spoke movingly of all the men the company had lost and then outlined the next day's operation for his officers. According to Calley, Medina told them that they should expect the "heaviest contact we had ever been in," that they would likely be outnumbered two to one, and that they "were going to search and probably also burn a lot." Calley later summarized what Medina went on to tell the men: "We were going to start at My Lai 4 and would have to neutralize My Lai 4 completely and not let anyone get behind us. Then we would move to My Lai 5 and make sure there was no one left in My Lai 5, and so on until we got into the Pinkville area. Then we would completely neutralize My Lai 1, which is Pinkville. He said it was completely essential that at no time [should] we lose our momentum of attack, because the two other companies that had assaulted the time in there before, had let the enemy get behind him, or had passed through the enemy, allowing him to get behind him and set up behind him, which would disorganize when he made his final assault on Pinkville. It would disorganize him, they would lose their momentum of attack, take heavy casualties, and would be more worried about their casualties than they would their mission, and that was their downfall. So it was our job this time to go through, neutralize these villages by destroying everything in them, not letting anyone or anything get in behind us, and move on to Pinkville." Significantly, Calley also claimed that Medina informed them that "all civilians had left the area, there were no civilians in the area. And anyone there would be considered enemies." (Hammer, 245 – 46).

Captain Medina has repeatedly denied giving an explicit order directing his men to kill everyone in the village, and given the fact that he was later placed on trial for his actions at My Lai, Calley's account may well be self-serving. Even so, the reports of several other members of Charlie Company, many of whom did not themselves face trial, support Calley's story in its essentials. Sergeant Hodges, for example, characterized Medina's briefing this way:

> "This was a time for us to get even. A time for us to settle the score. A time for revenge—when we can get revenge for our fallen comrades.
>
> The order we were given was to kill and destroy everything that was in the village. It was to kill the pigs, drop them into the wells; pollute the water supply; kill, cut down the banana trees; burn the village; burn the hootches as we went through it. It was clearly explained that there were to be no prisoners.

> The order that was given was to kill everyone in the village. Someone asked if that meant the women and children. And the order was: everyone in the village. Because those people that were in the village—the women, the kids, the old men—were VC. They were Viet Cong themselves or they were sympathetic to the Viet Cong. They were not sympathetic to the Americans. It was quite clear that no one was to be spared in that village." (Bilton and Sims, 98 – 99).

Similarly, Harry Stanley claimed, "Captain Medina had told us that the intelligence had established that My Lai 4 was completely controlled. He described the formations we were to use the following day and told us to carry extra ammunition. He ordered us to "kill everything in the village." The men in my squad talked about this among ourselves that night because the order to "kill everything in the village" was so unusual. We all agreed that Captain Medina meant for us to kill every man, woman, and child in the village." (Peers report).

At Calley's trial, no fewer than 21 men from Charlie Company would testify that Captain Medina ordered them to kill everyone in the village.

Barring the introduction of new physical evidence, the truth of just what Medina told his men that day will likely never be known, but at the very least, there is no indication that Henderson, Barker, or Medina issued any directives to distinguish civilian from Viet Cong property or to detain and protect noncombatants. In the absence of such orders, the men of Charlie Company had every reason to believe that the area was a Viet Cong stronghold, that any individuals they encountered there would be Viet Cong guerillas or Viet Cong sympathizers, and that their mission was to raze the village to the ground. They spent the night of March 15 "really psyched up," "scared," and ready to "wreak some vengeance on someone." (Peers report).

Obviously, it was a recipe for disaster.

**Chapter 6: The My Lai Massacre**

"There were some South Vietnamese people, maybe fifteen of them, women and children included, walking on a dirt road maybe 100 yards away. All of a sudden the GIs just opened up with M16s. Beside the M16 fire, they were shooting at the people with M79 grenade launchers... I couldn't believe what I was seeing." - Ronald Haeberle, a U.S. Army photographer at My Lai

Although the Son My operation promised to be intense, nothing about its earliest stages would have struck the men of Task Force Barker as particularly unusual. The members of Charlie and Bravo Companies rose early on the morning of March 16, gathered their supplies, and checked their weapons. Around 0715 hours, Captain Medina's command group, along with 1st and 2nd Platoons, boarded the transport helicopters that would carry them to their respective landing zones. "We felt as automobile racers do. A split second and I might hit the very edge of disaster," Calley recalled of the moment the helicopters lifted off. (Sack, 98 – 99) Each man carried about 60 pounds of gear, and since they were braced for a particularly intense encounter, many of them had packed extra ammunition.

Massive artillery barrages, designed to clear the landing zones, began before troops even hit the ground. The first troops from Charlie Company reached their assigned landing zone, just west of My Lai (4), around 0730, and they were joined by 3rd Platoon about 20 minutes later. The men secured the landing zone and then began advancing on My Lai (4), with 1st Platoon approaching from the south and 2nd Platoon from the north. 3rd platoon, tasked with moving in to destroy the village once it had been secured, held back with Captain Medina's command group.

**Picture of a helicopter landing near My Lai**

As they advanced, the men opened fire on fleeing villagers and likely hiding places, killing several, but despite their expectations, they did not encounter any enemy fire, mines, or booby traps. In fact, while the 48th Viet Cong Local Force Battalion had indeed made regular use of the villages, it had largely abandoned the area over the last few nights. A handful of genuine Viet Cong remained, and the few that were armed and attempting to escape were killed by helicopters circling the area. The villages, however, were almost entirely undefended, and instead of Viet Cong, they contained scores of civilians, largely old men, women, and children. Captain Koutoc's intelligence notwithstanding, few had left for the market that morning.

As they entered My Lai (4), 1st and 2nd Platoons began burning homes, rounding up villagers, and destroying caches of food, all of which was standard practice in a search and destroy operation. However, as they moved further into the village, their formations and lines of communication broke down amidst the smoke, noise, and thick vegetation. In the absence of effective operational control, and still awaiting the expected enemy fire, order broke down and soldiers began killing, mutilating and raping villagers.

It is difficult to reconstruct a coherent narrative of everything that happened at My Lai (4) that day, given that no single individual observed everything, physical evidence of the atrocities is limited and participants had every reason to minimize their own culpability after the fact. As a result, any narrative of the massacre is a tentative and partial reconstruction.

As 2nd Platoon advanced into the northwestern corner of My Lai (4), a crying woman came running out of a hut carrying a baby. According to Private Varnado Simpson, his commanding officer, Lieutenant Stephen Brooks, ordered him to shoot the woman. "Acting on his orders, I shot the woman and her baby." Reflecting on his story, which was later corroborated by Private First Class Dean Fields, Simpson commented, "And once you start, it's very easy to keep on. Once you start. The hardest—the part that's hard is to kill, but once you kill, that becomes easier, to kill the next person and the next on and the next one. Because I had no feelings or no emotions or no nothing. No direction. I just killed. It can happen to anyone. Because, you see, I wasn't the only one that did it. Hung 'em, you know—all type of ways. Any type of way you could kill someone, that's what they did. And it can happen." (Bilton and Sim, 7).

Soldiers allegedly tossed hand grenades into hovels and cut down children with semiautomatic fire. The leader of 1st Squad, 2nd Platoon allegedly shot several unarmed villagers after forcing them from their home, and Private Gary Roschevitz is reported to have fired at least two rounds from his M-79 grenade launcher into a group of prisoners consisting of men, women, and children. Roschevitz also allegedly used Private Simpson's M-16 to shoot at least five Vietnamese prisoners, including a woman and two girls being escorted by members of 1st Platoon. No one is reported to have resisted him, and, according to Private Johnnie Turnstal, he later bragged about the killing.

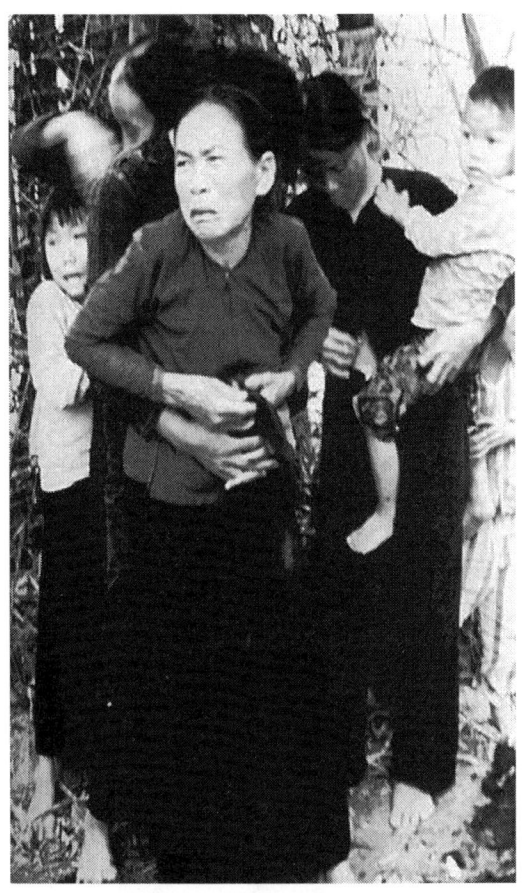

**A picture of detained women and children shortly before they were killed**

Around mid-morning, near the end of the My Lai operation, Specialist Fourth Class Thomas Partsch, of $2^{nd}$ Platoon sat down to note the following in a small diary he carried with him: "Got up at 0530 and we left 0715. We had nine choppers, two lifts. We started to move slowly though the village, shooting everything in sight, children, men, women, and animals. Some was sickening. Their legs were shot off and they were still moving. They were just hanging there. I think their bodies are made of rubber. I didn't fire a single round yet and didn't kill anybody, not even a chicken. I couldn't. We are now supposed to push two more villages. It is about 1000 hours and we are taking a rest before going in. We also got two weapons, one M-1 and a carbine." (Bilton and Sim, 116).

Private First Class Dean Fields, who served as Lieutenant Brooks' secretary, witnessed numerous atrocities. "They were doing a good job, and they were doing it, more or less, because they were told," he later recalled. "They were not out of control . . . After they left one hootch, they went to another hootch expecting to find more they could kill. I know for a fact they didn't hate to do it." (Allison, 39)

The scene where Lieutenant Calley's 1st Platoon entered the south of the village was even more gruesome if that was possible. Soldiers threw grenades into crowded huts, shot fleeing villagers, and herded survivors into ditches and opened fire. Amid the carnage, Privates Herbert Carter, Paul Medlo, Dennis Conti, and James Dursi collected a group of about 50 unarmed Vietnamese villagers, including women and children. According to Medlo and Conti, Lieutenant Calley, under pressure from Medina to advance more quickly through the village, approached, said "I want them killed," and ordered the men to shoot the prisoners. Medlo later reported that he and Calley began firing their M-16s into the group, both using several magazines.

Calley, accompanied by his radio operator, Specialist 4th Class Charles Sledge, then moved on to another group of detained men, women, and children. According to multiple witnesses, Calley, along with Medlo, Specialist 4th Class Allen Boyce, and Sergeant David Mitchell, started pushing the villagers into a nearby irrigation ditch. Calley then told Boyce and Medlo to open fire. At one point a young boy of perhaps two attempted to crawl out of the ditch. According to both Sledge and Private Harry Stanley, Calley picked the boy up, threw him back in, and then shot him. As more villagers were brought to the ditch, Calley ordered them thrown into the ditch and shot.

The killing apparently continued for a full hour. According to Stanley, "The people in the ditch kept trying to get out and some of them made it to the top, but before they could get away they were shot, too . . . There were a lot of people in the ditch with their heads blown open." (Peers report).

Around 0830, Captain Medina ordered Lieutenant Brooks and his platoon north of My Lai(4) to recover weapons from the bodies of two Viet Cong fighters killed by helicopters, and then further north to the village of Binh Tay. There, according to the Peers Inquiry, 2nd Platoon "continued the pattern of burning, killings, and rapes which it had followed inside My Lai (4)." At Binh Tay, Private First Class Leonard Gonzales reported rescuing a 16 year old girl who had been assaulted by another soldier: "If left on her own, someone would have killed her." Gonzales also reported encountering Private Roschevitz standing next to a pile of naked bodies of women and girls. According to Gonzales, Roshevitz claimed that he had ordered the women to undress, they had resisted, and he had fired at least two rounds of buckshot from his M-79 into the group. (Allison, 40) Around 0930, Brooks received orders from Captain Medina to stop shooting, burn all the structures in Binh Tay, collect the surviving villagers, and move them to the southwest.

When the first artillery barrage had begun, perhaps as many as 300 villagers, along with a small number of Viet Cong, began fleeing south toward Route 521. Troops from Charlie Company's 3rd Squad, 3rd Platoon who had been directed south to recover arms and equipment from Viet Cong killed earlier approached the group and opened fire, killing perhaps four "military aged males." According to Private Jay Roberts, an Army correspondent, and Sergeant Ronald Haeberle, a Signal Corps photographer—both circling the area in a helicopter—the squad also killed at least one woman hiding in a ditch in a rice field before turning back toward My Lai (4). (Haeberle).

Amidst all the carnage at My Lai, at least one genuine hero emerged: Warrant Officer Hugh Thompson, who spent the morning circling the village complex with his helicopter crew. Thompson had been throwing out smoke markers when he came upon wounded Vietnamese, standard procedure to help American medics find them and provide aid. However, he quickly noticed that instead of medics, the markers attracted soldiers who subsequently finished off the wounded villagers. On one occasion, Thompson and his crew, Specialists 4th Class Glenn Andreotta and Lawrence Colburn, located a wounded Vietnamese woman, marked her location, and then hovered nearby as a group of American soldiers led by Captain Medina himself approached. Thompson, Andreotta, and Colburn watched in horror as Medina, who later claimed that the woman made a sudden and threatening movement, shot and killed her.

**Thompson**

Later on, the helicopter crew came across a ditch that appeared to be filled with dead and wounded Vietnamese villagers. Thompson landed nearby and disembarked to investigate.

Approaching a sergeant—later identified as David Mitchell—Thomas requested to evacuate the wounded. "The only way to help them out is to put them out of their misery," Mitchell reportedly replied. The pair were then approached by a Lieutenant—later identified as Calley—who told Thompson to mind his own business. With nothing he could do, Thompson returned to his helicopter and took off. As he did, the crew saw Calley and Mitchell opening fire on the wounded villagers in the ditch. "He's not running this show; I'm the boss," Calley reportedly commented to Sledge. (Angers, 118 – 21).

Continuing on, Thompson and his crew passed a squad of soldiers approaching a group of Vietnamese villagers gathered together in a bunker. Determined to save the villagers, Thompson landed between the bunker and the soldiers, radioed a nearby helicopter gunship for backup, ordered Colburn and Andreotta to open fire to protect the villagers if necessary, and disembarked. Advancing on the officer, Lieutenant Brooks, Thompson declared that he would be relaying the villagers to safety. Brooks was irritated but made no move to stop him. Thompson then persuaded the terrified villagers to leave the bunker and board the gunship, which ferried them to safety southwest of the village. It took two trips, and while the helicopter was off transporting the first group, Thompson stood guard between Brooks' men and the remaining villagers. Later, Thompson, Colburn, and Andreotta returned to the ditch where they had encountered Calley and Mitchell earlier. In the ditch, they found a lone survivor, a girl of five or six, deeply in shock but still alive. Taking her back to their helicopter, they flew her to Quong Ngai City and an ARVN hospital. She survived.

By the time 3rd Platoon and Captain Medina's command group entered My Lai (4) from the west, the village was a hellish, chaotic mess of smoldering wrecks and mutilated corpses. Private Charles Glover and Sergeant John Smail both reported watching as Specialist 4th Class Fred Widmer, from Captain Medina's radio team, approached a boy of about five. The boy's face was badly wounded and one of his hands had been shot away. Widmer killed the boy with a burst from an M-16, later claiming that it had been an act of mercy. (Bilton and Sim, 128 – 29).

Sergeant Haeberle, the Signal Corps photographer, accompanied 3rd Platoon as it entered the village: "I knew it was something that shouldn't be happening but yet I was part of it. I think I was in a kind of daze from seeing all these shootings and not seeing any return fire. Yet the killing kept going on. The Americans were rounding up the people and shooting them, not taking any prisoners. It was completely different to my concept of what war is all about. I kept taking the pictures. That was my job as a photographer, to take pictures, a normal reaction I have with a camera, just picking up and keep on shooting, trying to capture what is happening around me. I feel sometimes that the camera did take over during the operation. I put it up to my eye, took a shot, put it down again. Nothing was composed. Nothing was prethought, just the normal reaction of a photographer. I was part of it, everyone who was there was part of it, and that includes the General and the Colonel flying above in their helicopters. They're all part of it. We all were. Just one big group." (Haeberle). Haeberle's photos, particularly the color shots he took with his private camera, would eventually play a key role in the Peers Inquiry.

Somewhat later, in the south of the village, Haeberle encountered a pair of unidentified soldiers with a small group of women and girls:

> "Just as soon as I turned away I heard firing. I saw people drop. They started falling on top of each other, one on top of another. I just kept on walking. I did not pay attention to who did it. By that time I knew what the score was. It was an atrocity. I felt I wanted to do something to stop this and, as we were going through the village, I asked some soldiers: "Why?" They more or less shrugged their shoulders and kept on with the killing. It was like they were fixed on one thing—search and destroy, and that meant killing civilians.
>
> "I noticed this one small boy had been shot in the foot. Part of the foot was torn off, he was walking toward the group of bodies looking for his mother. I put up my camera to my eye, I was going to take a photograph. I didn't notice a GI kneeling down beside me with his M-16 rifle pointed at the child. Then I suddenly heard the crack and through the viewfinder I saw this child flip over the top of the pile of bodies. The GI stood up and just walked away. No remorse. Nothing. The other soldiers had a cold reaction—they were staring off into space like it was an everyday thing, they felt they had to do it and they did it. That was their job. It was weird, just a shrug of the shoulder. No emotional reaction." (Haeberle).

Around 1030 hours, Major Charles Calhoun, Colonel Barker's executive officer, radioed Medina and ordered him to "stop the killing." Calhoun's motivations for the order remain unknown. Flying above the Son My complex in a helicopter, he may have seen the civilian carnage firsthand, and he may also have heard reports from other helicopter crews.

In any case, by the time the shooting finally stopped, the men of Charlie Company had killed, raped, and assaulted hundreds of civilians in My Lai (4). The exact number killed that day will never be known, but current best estimates are around 500. Throughout the entire operation, they found no weapons in the village and took no enemy fire. Officially, Colonel Barker reported 128 Viet Cong killed and three weapons captured (in the surrounding area), along with "approximately 10 – 11 women and children" inadvertently killed. His report was accepted and the task force was warmly congratulated by General Westmoreland.

War is a horrific, murderous undertaking, and by 1968 the war in Vietnam had already turned particularly ugly. Even in this context, however, the scale and sadism of the atrocities committed by American soldiers in the Son My village complex on March 16 are breathtaking. Primed to expect an intense firefight with the Viet Cong, the sort of head-on pitched battle they had been trained to fight, the men of Charlie Company had advanced on an unarmed, undefended village and laid it to waste in the most cruel and brutal manner imaginable. Reflecting, years later on his own culpability that day, Private Varnado Simpson commented, "How can you forgive? You know, I can't forgive myself for the things I did. How can I forget that—or forgive? There's a part of me that's kind and gentle. There's another part of me that's evil and destructive. There's more destructiveness in my mind than goodness. There's more wanting to kill or to hurt than to love or to care. I don't let anyone get close to me. The loving feeling and the caring feeling is not there." (Bilton and Sim, 8).

Truong Thi Le was an old woman when the producers of a documentary series interviewed her, but she lived at My Lai at the time of massacre. When she heard the artillery barrage, she hid in a rice field, and she was one of the lucky ones who survived the day unscathed. Nine of her family members were killed, and she told her interviewers, "I think of it all the time, and that is why I am old before my time. I remember it all the time. I think about it and I can't sleep. I'm all alone and life is hard and there's no one I can turn to for help. Then I think of it all the time. I'm always sad and unhappy and that's why I'm old. I think of my daughter and my mother, both of them dead. I think of it and I feel extremely sad. I won't forgive. I hate them very much. I won't forgive them as long as I live. think of those children, that small . . . those children still at their mothers' breasts being killed . . . I hate them very much . . . I miss my mother, my sister, my children. I think of them lying dead. I think of it and feel my insides being cut to pieces." (Bilton and Sims, 23).

## Chapter 7: The Aftermath of My Lai

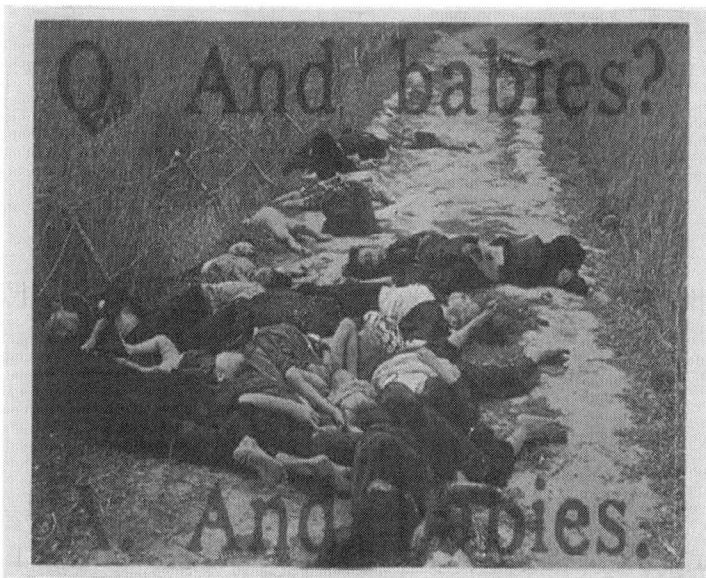

**An anti-war poster using a picture from the My Lai Massacre**

"Everyone in my family was killed in the My Lai massacre — my mother, my father, my brother and three sisters. They threw me into a ditch full of dead bodies. I was covered with blood and brains." – Tuyet, an 8 year old survivor

"We are calling for solidarity to defend peace, to defend life and to remind the world that it must never forget the massacre at My Lai." - Nguyen Hoang Son, vice governor of Quang Ngai

As soon as they returned to LZ Dottie on March 16, Hugh Thompson and his crew had reported the atrocities they had witnessed to their superiors. The allegations slowly made their way up the command chain, but most officers were skeptical and hesitant to risk their careers by leveling such inflammatory accusations at fellow soldiers. Suspiciously, all copies of Thompson's original after-action report have been lost. Similarly, when Jay Roberts, the brigade's correspondent, approached Colonel Barker with concerns about what he had witnessed, Barker reportedly replied "Don't worry about it," instructing Roberts to write a "good story."

Over the coming weeks, Task Force Barker continued its work more or less as normal, though on a few occasions, early reverberations of the events in My Lai were felt. On March 17, as a group of soldiers from 1st Platoon were making their way down the side of a hill near My Lai (4),

Private Paul Medlo stepped on a mine, which took his foot. As he was waiting to be evacuated, Medlo allegedly told Calley that the mine had been God's punishment for his crimes in My Lai. "You got yours coming!" he is reported to have shouted at Calley.

When word of Thompson's allegations reached him, Brigadier General George Young instructed Colonel Henderson to investigate any unusual occurrences during the Son My operation, an investigation the Peers Inquiry would later characterize as "little more than a pretense . . . subsequently misrepresented as a thorough investigation." Henderson questioned Thompson, a number of other pilots, and Captain Medina, but he failed to put any of them under oath or require written statements. Medina explained away the story that he himself had killed an unarmed civilian female in cold blood by asserting it was a mercy killing. As for reports of mass killings, he categorically denied that "American soldiers could do such a thing." Henderson also questioned a group of soldiers from Charlie Company, accepting at face value their denials that anything unusual had occurred during the operation. He did not question the soldiers individually.

On March 19, Henderson presented an oral report on his findings to Young and Major General Samuel Koster that essentially accepted Captain Medina's version of events. Henderson later claimed to have produced a written report as well, but no copy of such a report has ever been found. As a result, the Son My operation initially received positive coverage in the Americal Division's *News Sheet*, as well as in *Stars and Stripes* and the *New York Times*, the latter of which reported that 128 Viet Cong fighters were killed when "American troops caught a North Vietnamese force in a pincer movement" in Quang Ngai Province. (*New York Times*, March 17, 1968).

The matter might well have rested there had it not been for the conscience and persistence of Ronald Ridenhour, a young private from Arizona. Ridenhour was not in Charlie Company, but he was on friendly terms with several of its men after having trained with them in Hawaii. In the months following the Son My operation, Ridenhour heard a succession of grisly stories from soldiers who had taken part, including Charles Gruver, Michael Terry, William Doherty, and Michael Bernhardt. On the basis of some amateur sleuthing, Ridenhour concluded that something terrible had taken place at My Lai (4) and that official reports on the operation had either failed to unearth it or actively covered it up.

**Ridenhour**

At the same time, Ridenhour had considerable empathy for the men of Charlie Company, who he believed had been swept up into a strange and terrifying world. As he elaborated years later, "We were kids, eighteen, nineteen years old. I was twenty-one years old at the time. I was one of the oldest people around there among the common grunts. Most of [Charlie Company] had never been away from home before they went into the service. And they ended up in Vietnam, many of them because they thought they were going to do something courageous on behalf of their country. Here are these guys who had gone in and in a moment, in a moment, following orders, in a context in which they'd been trained, prepared to follow orders, they do what they're told, and they shouldn't have, and they look back a day later and realize they probably made the biggest mistake of their lives. [There were] only an extraordinary few people who were in those circumstances who had the presence of mind and the strength of their own character that would see them through. Most people didn't. And for most of them—people that I personally was just stunned to discover had made the wrong choice they did—they had to live with it. They have to live with it. And so do I. So do we all." (Bilton and Sims, 20).

Even so, the official non-response to the massacre played at Ridenhour's conscience. After completing his tour in late 1968 and returning to Arizona, Ridenhour agonized for several months over what to do. Finally, in February 1969, he decided to act. Ridenhour composed a long, detailed letter outlining everything he knew about atrocities committed during the Son My operation and sent copies to over 30 politicians and government officials, including Secretary of Defense Melvin Laird; Chairman of the Joint Chiefs General Earl Wheeler; Senators Barry

Goldwater, Eugene McCarthy, William Fulbright, and Ted Kennedy, and President Richard Nixon. While some recipients found Ridenhour's allegations incredible, his obvious sincerity won others over.

In all, Ridenhour's letters spurred a military investigation, a congressional investigation, a criminal trial, and, not least, a massive public outcry. Through multiple channels, Ridenhour's letter made its way to the Inspector General's Office in Washington. There, Colonel William V. Wilson, a former Green Beret newly attached to the office, happened to see the Ridenhour file and requested to be assigned to the case. "If the Pinkville incident was true, it was cold-blooded murder." he later explained. "I hoped to God it was false, but if it wasn't, I wanted the bastards exposed for what they'd done." (Wilson, 46).

Wilson proved to be a capable and energetic investigator. Within two months, he had interviewed not only Ridenhour (who he found "depressingly convincing") but also Terry, Bernhardt, Doherty, Gruver, Thompson, and Colburn. All corroborated Ridenhour's account.

In June 1969, the Army brought Lieutenant Calley to Washington to answer questions about his actions at My Lai (4), this time under oath. Calley, shocked to hear that he was under investigation for war crimes, requested counsel, refused to answer any questions, and then offered to testify in exchange for immunity. The investigators refused.

In August, Army investigators located Ronald Haeberle, who showed them color slides of the massacre consisting of the pictures he had taken on his personal camera. As horrible as Haeberle's pictures of the victims were, he had gotten rid of pictures that showed American soldiers actually in the process of killing women and children.

In November, concerned about rumors that a cabal of West Point graduates was conspiring to shield itself from blame, the Army turned the inquiry over to Lieutenant General William R. Peers, a stern World War II veteran who had worked his way up through the ROTC. The Peers Inquiry would ultimately interview about 400 witnesses and produce over 20,000 pages of testimony. To this day, the Peers Inquiry, completed in March 1970 and released publicly in 1974 after the My Lai courts-martial, remains the richest source for information on events surrounding the massacre.

**Peers**

The Peers Inquiry also resulted in a barrage of indictments. Lieutenant Calley was first, charged on September 5, 1969 with murdering 109 Vietnamese civilians. Next was Sergeant David Mitchell, on October 28, accused of assault to commit murder against 30 Vietnamese civilians.

In early 1970, the pace of indictments quickened. In January, Private Gerald Smith was indicted for murder and indecent assault and Sergeant Charles Hutto was charged with murder, assault, and rape. The following month, Captain Thomas Willingham of Bravo Company was charged with the unpremeditated murder of 30 civilians. On March 10, Captain Eugene Kotouc, Sergeant Kenneth Hodges, Sergeant Esquiel Torres, and Private Max Huston were all indicted for murder. They were followed by Private Robert T'Souvas, Private William Doerty, and

Sergeant Kenneth Schiel on March 25. Finally, on March 31, Captain Ernest Medina was accused of murdering 175 Vietnamese civilians. The Army suspected at least 19 others but could not charge them because they had already been honorably discharged, removing them from the jurisdiction of the military justice system.

Of course, if the men of Charlie Company would face judgment for their actions, so too would the military and the country as a whole. The news that an unknown Lieutenant had been indicted for murder did not immediately cause a stir in the national media, but in October 1969, a young Associated Press reported named Seymour Hersh received a tip that the Calley trial involved an alleged massacre in Vietnam. Hersh decided to investigate, and that November he produced a series of reports that shocked public and earned a Pulitzer Prize.

Public responses to news of the My Lai atrocities were incredibly varied. In November, before they were exposed to Haeberle's gruesome full-color photographs and the harrowing first-person narratives of many of the participants, many people simply refused to believe that the allegations could possibly be true. However, back in Washington, the *London Times* noted a strangely subdued response among those who were high-up and well-informed enough to know better: "There has been remarkably little reaction, either from the Congress or from anyone else. Congressional sources say . . . that senators have not reacted in public to the reports since they are not really so unexpected. People have known for a long time that Vietnam was an especially nasty war and that there have been plenty of incidents of brutality involving the American army. One more is merely one more." (*London Times*, November 26, 1969).

As the horrific details of the massacre began to leak out, however, a powerful sense of shock and disgust ran through sections of the American public. In December, the journalist Jonathan Schell, writing in the *New Yorker*, commented, "When others committed them, we looked on the atrocities through the eyes of the victims. Now we find ourselves, almost against our will, looking through the eyes of the perpetrators." (*New Yorker*, December 20, 1969). Like many others, Schell, who had actually reported from Quang Ngai province around the time of the massacre, felt that the horror of My Lai spoke to deeper truths about the American war effort in Vietnam: "There can be no doubt that such an atrocity was possible only because a number of other methods of killing civilians and destroying their villages had come to be the rule, and not the exception, in our conduct of the war." (Schell, 18).

In a similar vein, Senator George McGovern, already a firm opponent of the war, opined that "what this incident has done is tear the mask off the war." In waging war in Vietnam, the United States had "stumbled into a conflict where we not only of necessity commit horrible atrocities against the people of Vietnam, but where in a sense we brutalize our own people and our own nation . . . I think a national policy is on trial." (Hersh, 157 – 58).

**McGovern**

Supporters of the war effort, while often horrified and outraged at the atrocities, were more likely to see them as a glaring exception and the tragic actions of a few misguided criminals, not an illustration of the true nature of the conflict. For example, Army Secretary Stanley Rogers Resor advised the press, "What occurred at My Lai is wholly unrepresentative of the manner in which our forces conduct military operations in Vietnam . . . Our men operate under detailed directives which prohibit in unambiguous terms the killing of civilian noncombatants under circumstances such as those of My Lai." (Bilton and Sims, 13).

Others went further, arguing that no actual "massacre" had even occurred, and that Calley and his comrades were just scapegoats. Some even asserted that by rooting out a village of Viet Cong and Viet Cong sympathizers, Charlie Company had acted heroically. Senator Allen Ellender of Louisiana memorably stated that the victims in My Lai (4) had "got just what they deserved." When Captain Medina was called to testify before Congress, he was roundly applauded, and according to a *Time*–Louis Harris poll around this time, 65% of Americans agreed that My Lai was merely an "unfortunate part of war," not a criminal act.

**Ellender**

To the dismay of the My Lai prosecutors, the military courts-martial largely appeared to agree with this assessment. At David Mitchell's trial in Fort Hood, Texas, the judge, Colonel George R. Robinson, refused to allow testimony from anyone who had appeared before Edward Hebert's "Subcommittee on the My Lai Incident," decimating the ranks of the prosecution's witnesses. Mitchell was acquitted.

At the outset, Charles Hutto's trial at Fort McPherson, Georgia seemed more favorable to the prosecution. The judge, Colonel Kenneth Howard, did not rule out any of the prosecution's witnesses. Moreover, in his own statements to military investigators, Hutto had admitted that he "opened up" on a group of unarmed villagers, and that he "was firing at the people and shooting into the houses." "It was murder," he had declared. The defense team did not dispute any of this but argued that Hutto was poorly educated and mentally incapable of distinguishing legal from illegal orders. This line of argumentation contradicted both the Army's own *Law of Land Warfare* and the precedents set in the Nuremberg trials. Even so, the jury agreed, acquitting Hutto after less than two hours of deliberation.

Reconsidering their position following the Hutto verdict, the My Lai prosecutors decided to drop charges against all but three of their defendants: Captain Medina, Captain Kotouc, and Lieutenant Calley, whose trial was already underway. Medina and Koutoc were never convicted, but Calley's court martial, one of the most widely publicized trials in American history, opened in November 1970 and ran through March 1971. At times, both the relatively inexperienced prosecutors and Calley's disunited defense team seemed out of their depth. On the stand, Calley acknowledged that he had ordered his subordinates to "waste" a group of unarmed villagers, but he argued that he had merely been following Captain Medina's direct orders, something Medina denied in his own testimony. "I went into the area to destroy the enemy," Calley told the court. "They were enemy . . . It was a group of people that were the enemy, sir." Asked whether he had acted rightly, Calley replied, "I felt then and I still do that I acted as I was directed, and I carried out the orders that I was given, and I do not feel wrong in doing so, sir." (Hammer, 255 – 59).

After 79 hours of deliberation, the jury ruled that Calley was guilty of murdering at least 22 Vietnamese. Calley was sentenced to life in prison, yet the public response to Calley's conviction was almost wholly negative. Both war hawks who considered Calley a hero and "peaceniks" who considered him the scapegoat of an immoral war machine felt the sentence was unduly harsh. Indeed, according to a Gallup poll, only 11% of Americans even agreed that Calley was guilty. By this time, Calley had become something of a folk hero to a great many Americans, and "Free Calley" rallies sprang up spontaneously across the country. A 45 single called "The Battle Hymn of Lt. Calley," sung to the tune of "The Battle Hymn of the Republic," even became a hit for a Nashville record studio. The Veterans of Foreign Wars organized letter-writing campaigns and staged rallies in support of Calley, as did the American Legion.

Richard Nixon was unwilling to subvert the military justice system by pardoning Calley before his appeals had run their course, but he was still painfully sensitive to the direction of public opinion. Thus, he ordered that Calley be removed from the Fort Benning stockade and allowed to serve out his sentence under a fairly comfortable house arrest in his own apartment. In April 1974, his sentence was reduced to just 10 years by the new Army Secretary, Howard Callaway. This made Calley eligible for parole as early as November 1974. On November 19 of that year, Calley was paroled and his house arrest ended. He was once again a free man.

Calley wouldn't make a public statement of remorse for My Lai until 2009, and even then, he depicted himself as merely following orders: "There is not a day that goes by that I do not feel remorse for what happened that day in My Lai. I feel remorse for the Vietnamese who were killed, for their families, for the American soldiers involved and their families. I am very sorry....If you are asking why I did not stand up to them when I was given the orders, I will have to say that I was a 2nd lieutenant getting orders from my commander and I followed them—foolishly, I guess."

### Pictures of the Massacre Taken by Ronald Haeberle

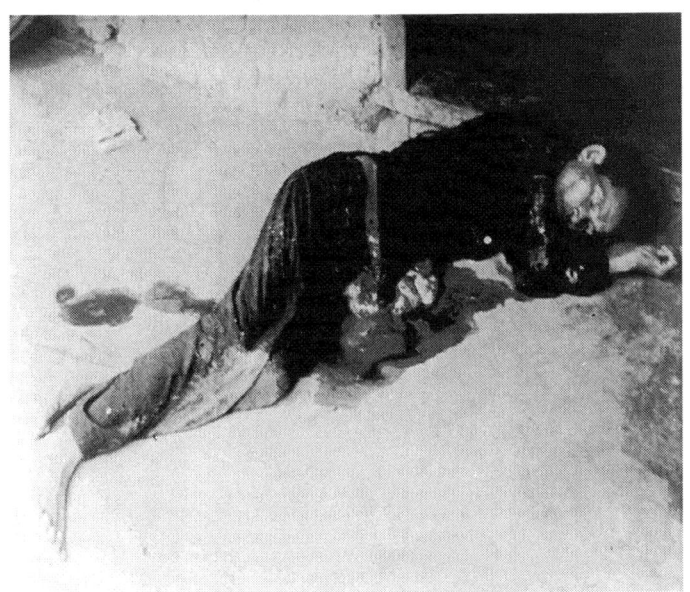

P-31  Unidentified Bodies Near Burning House (Haeberle Color #14A)

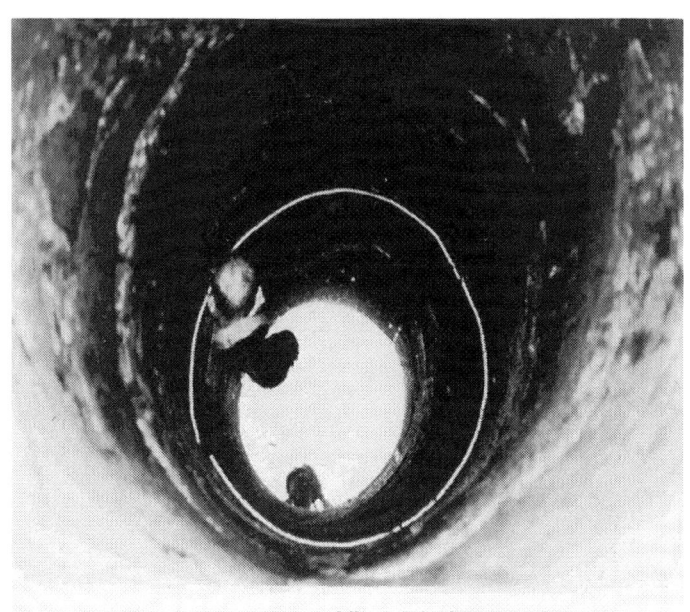

P-37  Unidentified Body in Well (Haeberle Color #154)

P-2  Unidentified Vietnamese Man (Haeberle B&W)

**Online Resources**

*The Vietnam Veterans Memorial: The History of Washington D.C.'s Vietnam War Monument* by Charles River Editors

**Bibliography**

Allison, William Thomas, *My Lai: An American Atrocity in the Vietnam War*, 2012.

Angers, Trent, *The Forgotten Hero of My Lai: The Hugh Thompson Story*, 1999.

Bilton, Michael and Kevin Sim, *Four Hours in My Lai*, 1992.

Caputo, Philip, *A Rumor of War*, 1988.

FitzGerald, Frances, *Fire in the Lake*, 1989.

Haeberle, Ronald, interview, 1992.

Hammer, Richard, *The Court-Martial of Lieutenant Calley*, 1971.

Hersh, Seymour, *My Lai 4: A Report on the Massacre and Its Aftermath*, 1970.

*London Times*

*New York Times*

*New Yorker*

Peers, William R., *The My Lai Inquiry*, 1979.

Sack, John, *Lieutenant Calley: His Own Story*, 1970.

Saltoli, Al, *Everything We Had*, 1981.

Schell, Jonathan, *Observing the Nixon Years*, 1990.

Sheehan, Neil, *A Bright Shining Lie*, 1990.

Summers, Col. Harry G., *On Strategy: A Critical Analysis of the Vietnam War*, 1984.

Westmoreland, General William, *A Soldier Reports*, 1976.

Widmer, Fred, interview, 1992.

Wilson, William V. "I Had Prayed to God that This Thing Was Fiction," *American Heritage*,

February 1990.

Young, Marilyn B. *The Vietnam Wars, 1945 – 1990*, 1990.

Made in the USA
Middletown, DE
24 October 2024